SHEWOLVES

by Sarah Middleton

ı|ıSAMUEL FRENCHıı

FOR PRODUCTION ENQUIRIES

United Kingdom and World
excluding North America
licensing@concordtheatricals.co.uk

020-7054-7298

North America
info@concordtheatricals.com
1-866-979-0447

Each title is subject to availability from Concord Theatricals, depending upon country of performance.

known or yet to be invented, including mechanical, electronic, digital, photocopying, recording, videotaping, or otherwise, without the prior written permission of the publisher. No one shall share this title, or part of this title, to any social media or file hosting websites.

The moral right of Sarah Middleton to be identified as author of this work has been asserted in accordance with Section 77 of the Copyright, Designs and Patents Act 1988.

USE OF COPYRIGHTED MUSIC

A licence issued by Concord Theatricals to perform this play does not include permission to use the incidental music specified in this publication. In the United Kingdom: Where the place of performance is already licensed by the PERFORMING RIGHT SOCIETY (PRS) a return of the music used must be made to them. If the place of performance is not so licensed then application should be made to PRS for Music (www.prsformusic.com). A separate and additional licence from PHONOGRAPHIC PERFORMANCE LTD (www.ppluk.com) may be needed whenever commercial recordings are used. Outside the United Kingdom: Please contact the appropriate music licensing authority in your territory for the rights to any incidental music.

USE OF COPYRIGHTED THIRD-PARTY MATERIALS

Licensees are solely responsible for obtaining formal written permission from copyright owners to use copyrighted third-party materials (e.g., artworks, logos) in the performance of this play and are strongly cautioned to do so. If no such permission is obtained by the licensee, then the licensee must use only original materials that the licensee owns and controls. Licensees are solely responsible and liable for clearances of all third-party copyrighted materials, and shall indemnify the copyright owners of the play(s) and their licensing agent, Concord Theatricals Ltd., against any costs, expenses, losses and liabilities arising from the use of such copyrighted third-party materials by licensees.

IMPORTANT BILLING AND CREDIT REQUIREMENTS

If you have obtained performance rights to this title, please refer to your licensing agreement for important billing and credit requirements.

SHEWOLVES was developed with young people in the Midlands. The play was first performed at Attenborough Arts Centre, Leicester on 29th April 2022 and then toured to Poplar Union, Lincolnshire YMCA, Derby Theatre, Nottingham Playhouse, Mansfield Palace Theatre, The Old Joint Stock and Pegasus Theatre, Oxford. *SHEWOLVES* was then performed at Theatre503, followed by a run at Pleasance, Edinburgh in partnership with Leicester Curve and Pleasance Futures from 3rd–29th August 2022. In 2023 *SHEWOLVES* toured the UK followed by a transfer to Southwark Playhouse.

LOU . . . . Harriet Waters (She/her)
PRIYA . . . . Gurjot Dhaliwal (She/her)

CREATIVE TEAM

WRITER | Sarah Middleton (she/her)
DIRECTOR | Hannah Stone (she/her)
SET AND COSTUME DESIGNER | Charlotte Henery (she/her)
LIGHTING DESIGNER | Anna Reddyhoff (she/her)
SOUND DESIGNER AND COMPOSER | Eleanor Isherwood (she/her)
DRAMATURG | Tilly Branson (she/her)
ASSOCIATE DIRECTOR | Keeley Lane (she/her)
FIRST TOUR ASSISTANT DIRECTOR | Octavia Nyombi (she/her)
NATIONAL TOUR ASSISTANT DIRECTOR | Hannah Brown (she/her)
TECHNICAL STAGE MANAGER | Steff Andrews (they/them)
FIRST TOUR PRODUCER | Courtenay Johnson for Carbon Theatre (she/her)

NATIONAL TOUR PRODUCER | Jake Orr for JOP (he/him)
OUTREACH COORDINATOR | Orla O'Connor (she/her)
NATIONAL TOUR OUTREACH PRODUCER | Andra Chelcea (she/her)
MARKETING SUPPORT | Charlotte Furness for Leviart Marketing (she/her)

FIRST TOUR PRESS | Michelle Mangan (she/her)
NATIONAL TOUR PRESS | Storytelling PR
DRAMA THERAPY CONSULTANT | Kath Akers (they/she)

Additional script support from Craig Gilbert and Matthew May
Script was developed with input from performers Safiyya Ingar,
Phoebe Brown, Claire Lams & Rose Quentin
Original Costume concepts by Hannah Sibai
Promotional video by Courtney Nettleford and Georgianna
Scurfield

Promotional Photos by Pamela Raith & Julian Hughes
Work in Progress photos by Julian Hughes

Wolfpack Creative Facilitators
Ria Ashcroft, Zoe Ambrose, Orla O'Connor, Sebbie Mudhai,
Octavia Nyombi and Evangeline Osbon.

CAST

GURJOT DHALIWAL | PRIYA

Gurjot is a recent graduate of The Royal Central School of Speech and Drama. She professionally debuted as the role of Yasmin in *Our White Skoda Octavia* by Shamser Sinha, 2021. Some of her other credits include: *Extremist* by Rikki Beadle-Blair, *A Dolls House* by Tanika Gupta and *The Wolves* by Sarah DeLappe.

HARRIET WATERS | LOU

Harriet has recently graduated from Mountview where she studied Musical Theatre. Credits whilst training include; Joyce Chilvers in *Betty Blue Eyes*, Violet in *Violet* and Rose in *Nell Gwynn*. Harriet has also played Taisie Scott, a returning role, in the ITV Drama *Scott and Bailey*. *SHEWOLVES* is Harriet's professional theatre debut.

CREATIVE TEAM

HANNAH STONE | DIRECTOR

Hannah is a director, theatre maker and producer. In 2019 she directed *Pinocchio* by Sarah Middleton for Nottingham Playhouse. In 2021 Hannah directed *Aidy the Awesome* commissioned by Curve Leicester which did a digital tour. "Fast moving & feisty – a comic heroine for girls to emulate" (The Stage) and recently toured across the UK.

In 2021 Hannah was Assistant Director on *Beauty and the Beast* at Nottingham Playhouse and 2022 was assistant on the 50th anniversary show, *71 Coltman Street* at Hull Truck.

In 2022 Hannah directed *SHEWOLVES* by Sarah Middleton which was chosen as one of the Stage's top shows at Edinburgh Fringe. She also directed a new version of *Goldilocks and the Three Bears* by Anna Wheatley at the Nottingham Playhouse where she is also an Associate Artist.

CHARLOTTE HENERY | SET AND COSTUME DESIGNER

Charlotte is a London-based set, costume and production designer, she is a graduate of the design course at the National Institute of Dramatic Art in Australia.

Previous Set and Costume Designer credits include: *The Moors, Three Sisters* (LAMDA); *Magdalene* (Arcola Theatre); *Rockets and Blue Lights* (National Theatre – Associate Designer to Laura Hopkins); *What Fatima Did...* Derby Theatre; *Silently Hoping* (VAULT Festival); *The Shy Manifesto* UK Tour.

ANNA REDDYHOFF | LIGHTING DESIGNER

Previous lighting design credits include: *A Little Night Music* (Avondale Theatre); *Vessel* UK Tour; *Copacabana* (Avondale Theatre); *The Strange case of Jekyll & Hyde* UK Tour; *A Strange Bit of History* UK Tour; *Giving up Marty, Fanny a New Musichall* (VAULT Festival); *Snow White* (Leicester Square Theatre); *Snow White & The Seven Dwarfs* (Bradford Alhambra – Associate LD to Matt Clutterham); *Albion in Flames* (Union Theatre); *The Lion, the Witch and The Wardrobe* (Garrick); *The Re-birth of Meadow Rain* (Edinburgh); *Pops* (Edinburgh); *Flinch* (The Old Red Lion); *Emilia* (Vaudeville – Associate LD to Zoe Spurr); *Heart* (VAULT Festival); *Tim Vine: Sunset Milk Idiot* (Hammersmith Apollo); *Sara Pascoe: Lads Lads Lads* (Wyndham's Theatre); *One Man, Two Guvnors* Lichfield Garrick; *Once Upon a Mattress* Lichfield Garrick.

ELEANOR ISHERWOOD | COMPOSER & SOUND DESIGNER

Ellie Isherwood is a freelance sound designer, composer, actor/musician and electronic music producer (BYFYN). She has worked on a vast array of projects including, site specific theatre, binaural audio tours, sound design for virtual reality roller coasters and short films, to name just a few! Ellie has also frequently worked as an assistant to top sound designers, Ben and Max Ringham. In addition to this she has recorded, produced and performed three EP's and five singles under the alias, BYFYN. Her most recent work includes Peut etre Theatre Company's adaptation of Lemony Snicket's *The Dark*, where Ellie wrote and performed an original score and played the role of The Dark.

TILLY BRANSON | DRAMATURG

Tilly Branson is a director, dramaturg, theatre-maker and creative producer with a particular interest in new writing and women's voices. Directing includes: *Gaze* by S. L. Page (Northern Stage); *Pepper and Honey* by Kristina Gavran (Notnow Collective); *Think of England* and *It Is Now* by Madeline Gould (Anonymous is a Woman); *Man To Man* by Manfred Karge (Mercury Theatre Colchester/Park Theatre London); *Entertaining Angels* by Brendan Murray (New Perspectives); and *End to End* (The Gramophones). Tilly has worked on scripts in development with writers and theatre-makers including Madeline Gould, Jane Upton, The Gramophones, Ava Hunt, and Kieran Spiers. She has been a judge for playwriting competitions for New Perspectives, Fifth Word and Nottingham Playhouse, and is a script reader for Fifth Word.

KEELEY LANE | ASSOCIATE DIRECTOR

Keeley is a theatre and screen director and performer with a passion for storytelling, new writing, classics reimagined and creating theatrical experiences that can stretch beyond the traditional stage. Her enthusiasm lies with stories with female protagonists or where women have a key role in the story.

Recent credits include, as Director: *Glow* Buglight Theatre 2022; *Scriptworks* Cast Doncaster. As Associate Director: *The Miami Showband Story (*Grand Opera House/Gaiety Theatre GBL Productions). As Assistant Director: *Fairy Poppins* & *The Naughty Winter Ghost* (Leeds Playhouse).

OCTAVIA NYOMBI | ASSISTANT DIRECTOR

Octavia is a performance artist and maker, with a First Class Drama Degree from De Montfort University. She has notably performed in *Queer Upstairs* at the Royal Court and starred in Travis Alabanza's film *Burgerz and Chips*. She is Artistic Director of the queer, feminist company Category: Peach. Currently developing *Pol-Spiracy*, an urgent, roaring new play about Poland, previously performed as part of Barrel Organ's LIVE Programme and Curve Theatre's New Work Festival. Her leadership skills are recognised at Nottingham Playhouse, where she is a Lead Practitioner facilitating workshops, Chairing their Youth Board and setting up their Queer Arts Collective.

HANNAH BROWN | NATIONAL TOUR ASSISTANT DIRECTOR

Hannah Brown is new in the industry after studying and performing in Chapter 4 Youth Theatre until 2017. During this time she appeared in shows such as *A Letter to Lacey* by Catherine Johnson (2014) as *Kara 1,* performed at Mansfield Palace Theatre and Sheffield Crucible. Hannah also starred in *The Boy Preference* by Elinor Cook (2015); *I'm Spilling My Heart Out Here* by Stacey Gregg (2016), and *Zero for the Young Dudes!* by Alistair McDowall (2017), all of which performed at Mansfield Palace Theatre and Derby Theatre as a participant of National Connections. Hannah studied Performing Arts at West Nottinghamshire College where she played Lulu in Mark Ravenhill's *Shopping and F*cking*, Jocasta in Steven Berkoff's adaptation of *Oedipus*, and Rudenko in *The Grain Store*, a hard hitting play about the Holodomor in Ukraine written by Natal'ia Vorozhbit.

Since completing her studies, Hannah has worked as stage crew at Mansfield Palace Theatre since 2017 and has recently started an apprenticeship as a Creative Venue Technician within her home theatre. Most recently she has acted as the Trainee Assistant Director on the reboot of *SHEWOLVES* by Sarah Middleton, directed by Hannah Stone; a new play for teenagers developed with and for young women in 2020 supported by Mansfield Palace Theatre, Derby Theatre and New Art Exchange. She hopes for this to just be the start of a bright future in directing and creating new theatre.

STEFF ANDREWS | TECHNICAL STAGE MANAGER

Credits include: *Cinderella* (Harrow Arts Centre); *Upswing Aerial, Seasons, Happy's Circus, Don Giovanni* (The Merry Opera Company); *Aladdin* (Castle Theatre); Reasons to Stay Alive (ETT); Grange International Opera Festival, *Animalcolm* (Story Pocket Theatre); *The Enourmous Present* (Pied Piper Theatre Company); *Pot* (Rua Arts); *Tiddler and Other Terrific Tales* (Freckle Productions); *Little Red Riding Hood* (Moon on a Stick Theatre Company); *Madame Butterfly, Carmen* (Broadway Theatre, Peterborough); *The Pirates of Penzance* (Heritage Opera).

COURTENAY JOHNSON | PRODUCER

Courtenay is an independent arts and cultural producer based in Northamptonshire. Her work focuses on producing inclusive, female-centred work alongside larger arts & heritage projects. Courtenay runs Carbon Theatre and is Executive Producer of 60 Miles by Road or Rail. Her previous projects include: *60 Miles by Road or Rail* by Ryan Leder, directed by Andy Routledge at Royal & Derngate, Northampton, 22-25 September 2021; *Seedling* by Helen Crevel with Anne Langford, an audio installation in Grosvenor Centre, Northampton; *My Sensory Adventures* (2020-21), an inclusive sensory project which included free video activities, resources, original songs & free packs for families to enjoy at home; and, *When We Died* by Alexandra Donnachie premiered at VAULT Festival 2020 and the filmed version of the production premiered digitally as part of Edinburgh Festival Fringe 2021.

SHEWOLVES PRODUCTIONS

Led by director Hannah Stone and writer Sarah Middleton, Shewolves Productions are based in the Midlands and make new writing that centres women. We work with professionals and communities to create funny, uplifting plays and projects that tell stories about complex women who have agency within their lives.
www.weareshewolves.co.uk
Twitter: @SHEWOLVES__

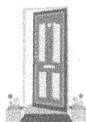

ARTS COUNCIL ENGLAND
Supported using public funding by
LOTTERY FUNDED

COMMUNITY FUND

Nottingham Women's Centre
come on in

CHARACTERS

LOU – (14)
PRIYA – (14)

SETTING

The story takes place in a suburb of Derby, in the East Midlands, and in the Peak District.

For Andy, Elliot, Jess, Katy, Laura, LJ and Rob.
With whom I found my voice.

And in memory of the brilliant Phoebe Brown.

Prologue

(A searchlight swings around, eventually finding **PRIYA** *(14) and* **LOU** *(14).*

BOTH. Shewolves, Shewolves!

*(***LOU*** lifts the gun.)*

LOU. SHEWOLVES MOTHERFUCKERS!!!

*(***LOU*** fires the gun. Lights strobe and music blasts* as she fires it. Blackout.)*

---

* A licence to produce SHEWOLVES does not include a performance licence for any third-party or copyrighted music. Licensees should create an original composition or use music in the public domain. For further information, please see Music Use Note on page iii.

One

*(Outside the school gates. **PRIYA** is there. She's wearing a large backpack. **LOU** arrives and begins setting up a climate change protest. She props up a sign reading 'Skolstrejk för Klimatet!' and then takes out a roll of gaffer tape. **PRIYA** is hovering.)*

PRIYA. *(To **LOU**.)* Skipping school? Me too.

LOU. I'm not skipping school, I'm saving the planet.

PRIYA. Why?

LOU. What?!

PRIYA. Why you saving it?

LOU. Because if sea levels keep rising it'll become inhospitable to human life.

And we'll become extinct.

*(**PRIYA** is lost.)*

It means we'll all die.

PRIYA. What's the point? We're all gonna die anyway.

LOU. Wow.

*(**LOU** cuts a length of gaffer tape.)*

PRIYA. If I was as smart as you, I wouldn't bother. I'd invent stuff, live in a mansion and be a billionaire.

LOU. Money won't save you when the planet's under water.

(Pause.)

PRIYA. But Rose survived in Titanic. She was minted and she survived.

LOU. What?

PRIYA. Leonardo DiCaprio was poor, so he died.

LOU. I don't think he died because he was poor.

PRIYA. I think he did.

LOU. He died because he didn't fit on the raft.

PRIYA. Exactly.

> (**PRIYA** *hovers and watches* **LOU**.*)*

> (**LOU** *sticks the tape over her mouth and stands silently with the sign.)*

LOU. Do you want something?!

PRIYA. Just seeing what you're doing.

> (**LOU** *rips off the tape to speak. It hurts.)*

LOU. I'm meant to be doing a silent protest. I'm sacrificing my education on Fridays until the government makes environmental pledges.

PRIYA. That's a posh way of saying you're skiving, isn't it.

LOU. It's not skiving, it's 'Skolstrejk för Klimatet?'

'Fridays for future'?!

...the Greta thing?

PRIYA. Why d'you have to be silent?

LOU. I tried shouting last week. I got a final warning and a sore throat.

PRIYA. You got a final warning?!

LOU. From Mr Davies. And I got grounded. But Julie's away this week, so I'm back.

PRIYA. Who's Julie?

LOU. My Mum.

PRIYA. What, she left you on your own?!

LOU. Just 'til Wednesday.

PRIYA. Sick! You gonna have a house party?

LOU. What?!

PRIYA. Can I come?

LOU. No. No! I need to carry on now. If you're not striking, you need to go in.

PRIYA. I'm striking.

LOU. This isn't skiving, Priya, it's a proper political –

PRIYA. I know that! ...I'm eco!

LOU. Are you?!

PRIYA. Yeah! Like Greta.

LOU. Do you even know who Greta is?

PRIYA. Yes! She's mates with my cousin, I've been to Five Guys with her.

LOU. With Greta Thunberg?

This is serious. And the tape's very painful, actually.

PRIYA. I've waxed my lip before!

LOU. That's not the same! You have to be a serious activist to join in.

(Pause.)

And I really don't think you went to Five Guys with Greta Thunberg. She's vegan for a start –

PRIYA. She had a veggie patty, okay?!

LOU. I think I would know if Greta came to Derby.

PRIYA. Well, maybe it was a different Greta.

> (**LOU** *looks at her.*)

Greta's a dead popular name, actually.

LOU. You need to go in.

PRIYA. I don't wanna go in, I –

LOU. It's not for you!

PRIYA. Fucks sake.

> (**PRIYA** *puts her hood up.*)

LOU. Look. I'm sorry. That was harsh. You can join in if you really want to.

Here you go.

> (**LOU** *offers her the gaffer tape.*)

PRIYA. I don't need it.

LOU. But it's a silent protest –

PRIYA. Nobody listens to me anyway.

> (**PRIYA** *leaves.* **LOU** *watches her go.*)

> (**LOU** *sighs and sticks the tape back over her mouth.*)

Two

(Evening. **LOU***'s house.* **PRIYA** *rings the doorbell. It plays a holy tune.* **LOU** *opens the door.)*

PRIYA. Can I come in?

LOU. Did you follow me home?

PRIYA. No! ...well, not in a weird way.

LOU. How is it not weird to follow someone home from school?

PRIYA. It's an emergency.

*(***LOU** *is not convinced.)*

Can I come in?

It's cold.

LOU. Where's your coat?

PRIYA. If you leave me out here and I get hit by a deliveroo driver and mangled up, it'll be your fault and you'll have to visit me in hospital for ever.

LOU. That is statistically very unlikely.

PRIYA. You'd have to buy me so many grapes. And probably wipe my bum.

LOU. What do you want?

PRIYA. Fine. I need somewhere to stay for a few nights. Your mum's away, right? So nobody will know. It's chilled!

LOU. Izzy's?

PRIYA. Izzy's mum works for social services, so I can't go to her's.

LOU. You can't just stay over for no reason!

PRIYA. I have a reason.

LOU. It'd better be good. Julie's super strict.

PRIYA. She's not even here!

LOU. We still have rules. Tell me what's going on and I'll think about it.

> (**LOU** *folds her arms and looks at* **PRIYA**.*)*

PRIYA. Fine... it's family stuff.

LOU. Like what?

PRIYA. I really don't wanna talk about it.

LOU. Then how do I know you aren't making it up?

PRIYA. Trust me, you couldn't make up the shit that happens at my house.

> (**LOU** *threatens to close the door.*)

Alright, I've run away from home.

I just. I need somewhere to stay, OK?

LOU. Priya –

PRIYA. So I don't go extinct.

> *(Pause.)*

> (**LOU** *lets* **PRIYA** *in.*)

Three

*(Later that evening. **LOU***'s room. They are doing homework. **PRIYA** is looking around the room. **LOU** finishes her essay.)*

LOU. Done. I'm getting a Pop-Tart. D'you want one?

PRIYA. Bring them out!

*(**LOU** goes to the kitchen to prepare the Pop-Tarts.)*

LOU. *(Off-stage.)* Please don't break anything!

*(**PRIYA** explores the room for a few minutes.)*

(She sees how perfect everything is.)

(She feels lost.)

PRIYA. Can I go on your phone?

LOU. *(Off-stage.)* Do you not have one?!

PRIYA. Not any more.

LOU. *(Off-stage.)* ...OK?

*(**PRIYA** goes on **LOU***'s phone.)*

(She calls her mum.)

(She waits.)

(No answer.)

*(**LOU** comes back in with two plates of Pop-Tarts and two napkins.)*

PRIYA. This is posh.

(Picks up the Pop-Tart.)

That's hot, its hot!

LOU. It's toasted, you have to wait!

PRIYA. OK. I'm not good at waiting, but to be fair this smells peng so I'll try.

(**PRIYA** *watches her Pop-Tart cool down.*)

LOU. I didn't mean to be harsh when I said don't break anything.

PRIYA. That's OK. I am clumsy. If life was a sweet shop, I'd be fizzwizz.

LOU. That's poetic.

PRIYA. You'd be a strawberry lace.

(**PRIYA** *smiles at* **LOU**.)

LOU. Have you finished your homework?

PRIYA. Nah. Education's not really for me.

LOU. OK… what do you want to do then? With your life?

PRIYA. Nobody in my endz wants to "do anything with their life". Everybody just wants to get paid. It's not a bad thing. You're gonna cure cancer or something – you'll live in a big house, go on posh holidays and see the world and everything.

LOU. We'll see.

PRIYA. And I'll be on benefits. Or *Love Island*. Reckon benefits is gonna be better for my mental health though. People lose their minds on *Love Island*.

(**LOU** *blows on her Pop-Tart.* **PRIYA** *copies.*)

LOU. Who were you calling?

PRIYA. No-one. When?

LOU. When I was making the Pop-Tarts. You rang someone.

PRIYA. I was just checking insta. I've got one thousand, two hundred and forty eight followers.

LOU. I don't have insta.

PRIYA. Oh my God, why not?

LOU. Because social media isn't a substitute for activism.

PRIYA. It's fun though.

(**PRIYA** *takes a bite out of the Pop-Tart.*)

This is piff! I'm gonna sue my mum, she's such a basic bitch for never getting these in.

LOU. How does that make her a basic bitch?

PRIYA. Mums are meant to look after you and put you first and buy you cool things, she just...

(**PRIYA** *eats more Pop-Tart.*)

Can we do something fun now? It's Friday night! We're meant to be enjoying ourselves! Have you ever had a sleepover before? Cos there's no face masks or nail stuff or anything!

LOU. Well I didn't exactly have time to prepare.

PRIYA. Don't panic. I'm like a professional sleepover person. I can stay awake all night and not even get tired.

(**LOU** *is scared.*)

And my mum does nails and stuff, so I'm sick at beauty.

LOU. OK?

PRIYA. What do you do at the weekend? Tell me you have fun sometimes.

LOU. ...not telling you.

PRIYA. Why not?

LOU. You'll laugh!

PRIYA. Is it rude?

LOU. No.

PRIYA. Is it porn?

LOU. What?! No!

PRIYA. You dirty bitch!

LOU. I'm learning how to use a 3D printer!

You can print anything you want with it.

PRIYA. Like what?

LOU. I'm making a USB cable organiser.

PRIYA. You can print anything in the world and you're making a USB cable organiser?!

LOU. It's a trial. I'll make bigger things later.

PRIYA. How much did it cost? The 3D machine?

LOU. My mum bought it –

PRIYA. Your mum gets you so much stuff!

LOU. Only if its educational.

PRIYA. Or Pop-Tarts!

LOU. I get the Pop-Tarts, Julie just leaves me her credit card when she's away.

PRIYA. Julie is a legend.

LOU. You don't know Julie. I mean, she'd be lovely to you, but...

It's a church thing, she loves a lost cause.

(*Pause.*)

PRIYA. Do you want me to pluck your monobrow?

Might be fun.

Four

(The next morning. The living room. **PRIYA** *is eating another Pop-Tart.)*

LOU. Wildfires are burning through California, and temperatures are going up every single year!

PRIYA. Your eyebrows look so much better now. There's a proper gap in the middle. I'm proud of you.

LOU. Look at this –

*(***LOU*** *searches on her phone.)*

PRIYA. I don't wanna see any more of them skinny polar bears. Puts me off my Pop-Tart.

LOU. But do you get it now?

PRIYA. Squeaky bum time, innit.

(She makes a tiny shape with her finger and thumb and wiggles it.)

Like when you're scared and your bum-hole goes squeak-squeak?

LOU. Oh.

PRIYA. Have you never had that? How is your life so nice?!

LOU. I have had a squeaky bum-bum!

PRIYA. Squeaky bum-TIME.

LOU. I got sixty-four percent in biology once and Julie had a meltdown. I had the poorly poos all week and I thought I was gonna die.

PRIYA. Poorly poos?

LOU. Yep.

PRIYA. The shits?

LOU. Yeah. And she didn't speak to me for a week. I cried. Well nearly – I don't believe in crying so I did my Greta scowl instead.

PRIYA. Your what?!

LOU. My Greta scowl. Like Greta at the UN.

> *(She scowls like Greta.)*

Try it.

> *(She shows* **PRIYA** *exactly how to do it.)*

LOU. See? Powerful.

> *(The post arrives.)*

PRIYA. Post!

LOU. I'll get it.

> *(**LOU** gets the post.)*

> *(**PRIYA** returns to the Pop-Tart.)*

PRIYA. I could eat these all day. How many Pop-Tarts do you think I could eat before I puked? Why are they called Pop-Tarts?

> *(She has fun saying the words Pop-Tarts.)*

Pop. Pop-Tarts. Popo Tartos. Poppy Tarts. PTs.

> *(**LOU** opens a letter. She reads it.)*

Lou, why d'you think Pop-Tarts are called Pop-Tarts?

LOU. I've been excluded from school.

PRIYA. As if! What for?

LOU. Climate strike.

PRIYA. Hang on, does this mean you get time off?

LOU. It's a permanent suspension. I've been expelled!

PRIYA. Sick!

LOU. NOT sick! It says it goes on my permanent record. So I won't be able to go to university and study 3D design, or contribute to the climate fight, and then when the sea levels rise and the forests are burning down, I'll know that I didn't do enough and – and –

    (**LOU** *starts panicking.*)

And – and – Julie! Oh my God, Julie will never speak to me again. She went mental when I got a warning for protesting, we had this massive, horrible argument and she kept saying education was more important than climate change, and that she wasn't even sure climate change was real – she didn't listen – she never listens – and now she's going to disown me!

PRIYA. Whoa, chill out, let me see.

    (**LOU** *shows her the letter.*)

Mr Davies. What a Karen.

LOU. "Louise has demonstrated extremist views"! We have passed records of her 'protests' on to the police, who will be in touch should they consider it appropriate.'

PRIYA. Oh my days, you're gonna get arrested!

LOU. D'you think?

PRIYA. You're an extremist!

LOU. Am I?!

PRIYA. I don't mean this in a bad way but if you get sent to juvie, I think you'll actually die quite soon. My cousin said they do human sacrifices in there and voodoo and stuff.

LOU. Really?

(**PRIYA** *nods solomnly.*)

Oh my God! I'm going to get arrested and die in juvie, and I'll never get to meet Greta, or speak in the House of Commons or win the Nobel Peace Prize, and my whole life will have been a HORRIBLE WASTE!

(**LOU** *is crying but she's trying to scowl instead. It's a lot.*)

PRIYA. Are you having a breakdown?

LOU. I'm scowling!

(**LOU** *panics more and scowls more.*)

PRIYA. Shall I show you how to do rainbow breaths? You're going a bit purple.

(**PRIYA** *shows* **LOU** *how to do rainbow breaths. When she breathes in her hands go upwards, and when she breathes out they make a rainbow downwards.* **LOU** *does the movements but is not calm. They continue whilst talking.*)

LOU. Every time I try and do something good, I get a detention or a verbal warning or expelled or arrested! I can't do it any more! It is STRESSFUL!!!!

PRIYA. You're not doing the rainbow breaths right! Do it like this –

(**LOU**'s *phone pings and she reads a text.*)

LOU. OH MY GOD Julie's coming home early! She knows.

PRIYA. What?

(**LOU** *hands her the phone.*)

LOU. What am I gonna do? She's going to rip my head off!

PRIYA. Shall I show you some karate? I'm a black belt, I can do a drop kick.

LOU. I can't drop kick my mum.

PRIYA. You can if she tries to rip your head off.

Just go to a mate's house, 'til she chills out. Sammy's?

LOU. I'm not going to Sammy's. Where am I gonna go?! Oh my God.

PRIYA. Can I stay here? While you're gone?

LOU. No. No, you'll have to go home.

PRIYA. But you said Julie would be nice to me!

LOU. Not if I'm missing when she gets back! She'll probably think you've murdered me and buried me under the patio!

I'm going to have to run away.

And you'll have to go home.

PRIYA. That's not – I can't.

　　　　(*Pause.*)

We could run away together!

LOU. Together? Let's think about this properly. Where can we go?

　　　　(*They think.*)

PRIYA. What about the Pentagon roundabout? The bit where the travellers live in the middle.

LOU. The Travelodge at Toby Carvery?

PRIYA. Kaylen's mum works there, she might get us a discount.

LOU. No, we can't be spotted, we need somewhere where no-one will find us.

PRIYA. Have you seen *Celebrity Hunted*? Whenever they hide near their house, the police always find them after like an hour. Even if they have a wig on.

LOU. Oh my God we can't do this. I don't even own a wig.

PRIYA. Believe in yourself! I bet Greta would run away.

LOU. Would she?!

PRIYA. Yeah. Kinda like a protest. But better. We could go somewhere far away.

LOU. Out of Derby...?

PRIYA. Exactly.

(*They think.*)

Butlins!

LOU. What's that?

PRIYA. I swear to God you've been living in an egg. It's a seaside holiday thing – it's sick! They do talent competitions and all the staff are on drugs!

LOU. No, we need somewhere remote! No staff, no drugs.

Oh my God, the Peak District!

PRIYA. Where's that?

LOU. You don't know where the Peak District is?

(**PRIYA** *shrugs.*)

It's where Robin Hood hid with his merry men. And women.

We could hide out in the wild. Like outlaws.

PRIYA. Cool!

LOU. We could live in the trees or maybe in a bothy or a barn?

PRIYA. Sick!

LOU. And then, when we eventually come home, nobody will care that I got expelled cos they'll just be happy we survived.

And your family stuff might have calmed down.

And then we'll both be able to go home.

PRIYA. You swear?

LOU. I swear. On Greta and the polar bears.

PRIYA. OK boss.

LOU. OK.

PRIYA. We need a name. For our mission.

LOU. Like 'Extinction Rebellion'.

PRIYA. But catchy.

LOU. Feminist Robin Hoods?

PRIYA. Umm?

LOU. Hood Squad?

(**PRIYA** *looks appalled.*)

No, that sounds like a movie, this is real!

Something about surviving.

PRIYA. And not going extinct.

LOU. Exactly! Arctic werewolves?

PRIYA. Nearly-dead polar bears?

LOU. Hungry badgers –

PRIYA. Wolves that are dribbling!!

LOU. Wolves... the Shewolves?

PRIYA. Yeah! What's a shewolf?

LOU. Just a wolf that's female. They live in a pack and they survive in the wild. And they're badass.

PRIYA. Shewolves. Yeah.

LOU. If we get in trouble and we need the pack, we howl, OK? That's our signal. Let's try it.

BOTH. One, two, three –

(They throw their heads back and howl.)

Five – A

(Music.*)

*(**LOU** reads a list and **PRIYA** carries everything, loading up with tins of baked beans, pepper spray, walking boots, toilet paper, maps, enormous backpacks etc. **LOU** pays with Julie's credit card whilst **PRIYA** inspects a She-wee.)*

LOU. Priya!

PRIYA. It's called a She-wee, it's like a camping dick!

---

* A licence to produce SHEWOLVES does not include a performance licence for any third-party or copyrighted music. Licensees should create an original composition or use music in the public domain. For further information, please see Music Use Note on page iii.

Five – B

*(**PRIYA** calls her mum again. Her mum doesn't answer.)*

Five – C

(They enter Julie's walk-in wardrobe.)

PRIYA. Its like a Narnia for clothes!

LOU. Focus! We need expedition outfits.

(They find vintage ski suits.)

Thank you Julie.

Five – D

PRIYA. Race you.

> *(They put the ski suits on.)*

We look banging, like milfs from the olden times!

LOU. … I look like a maggot.

Five – E

(They switch off the phone, and set off on their mission.)

LOU. Phone off. Untraceable.

(They put on sunglasses to disguise themselves.)

PRIYA. Into the wild, bitches.

Six

(*Hope Valley, in the Peak District.*)

(**PRIYA** *waves to the taxi as it leaves.*)

PRIYA. Wave to the taxi guy. He's a babe.

(*They loudly pretend to be doing D of E.*)

LOU. "I'm so excited for our D of E Expedition!"

PRIYA. OK he's gone.

(*They take off the shades.* **PRIYA** *sees the countryside for the first time.*)

Wow. WOW! We're doing it! The Peak District.

(**LOU** *unpacks the OS map.*)

(*She has fun saying the words 'Peak District'.*)

Peak. Peeeeak. Peaky. Peak. The Peak District. The P to the D. The P in the D.

The PD.

(**PRIYA** *farts silently.*)

LOU. Map.

PRIYA. Can a fart go back into a bum-hole?

Lou! Do you think if you fart in a ski suit it will ever escape? Or will it eventually find your bum-hole and go back in there...?

(**LOU** *opens out the map.*)

It's a good question!

LOU. Really good, gold star.

(**LOU** *studies the map.*)

PRIYA. I packed a lot of beans, so maybe we'll find out.

LOU. OK, we're in the Hope Valley which is...

PRIYA. Can I go on your phone?

LOU. No! If we switch it on we'll be traceable, and they'll find us in five minutes. *Celebrity Hunted*?!?!?!

PRIYA. Oh yeah... Lemme see this map then. Hope Valley.

(*She finds it immediately.*)

There it is. Come on!

(*They set off.* **PRIYA** *inhales.*)

I like it here. It smells different. I swear there's more air.

Unless I've just got dead big nostrils? Or hairy nostrils, are my nostrils too hairy, should I wax them?!

(*They enter a field. There's a bull.* **PRIYA** *freezes.*)

Why is that cow staring at us?

LOU. Which cow?

PRIYA. Look at its eyelashes, its like a drag queen cow. It's not a bull is it?!

LOU. Stop talking so loud, cows don't like loud stuff.

PRIYA. Don't bulls eat people?

LOU. No, they're herbivores.

PRIYA. Why is it on its own?

Where are its cow friends?

LOU. We need to keep going.

PRIYA. I hope you know what you're doing here with this animal stuff, because I have not been to biology since Year Seven.

>   *(The cow takes a step towards them.)*

And I don't think a drop kick would protect us from a bull.

LOU. It's not a bull. It's a heifer.

>   *(**PRIYA** can't move.)*

It's not going to hurt you. Come on.

PRIYA. If I die from a bull attack I'm gonna come back and haunt you so bad!

>   *(The bull walks towards them.)*

Why is it walking, why is it walking towards us like that?

LOU. I don't know, I'm not David Attenborough!

>   *(**LOU** looks at the cow.)*

Oh.

PRIYA. Lou?

LOU. I think it is a bull.

PRIYA. What?

>   *(The bull charges at them.)*

LOU. RUN!!

PRIYA. Wait for me!!

LOU. RUN FOR YOUR LIFE!

PRIYA. YOU SAID IT WAS A HEIFER!

*(**PRIYA** screams and runs across the field, **LOU** catches up and they pile into a heap in the next field, face down and covered in backpacks.)*

Seven

*(The aftermath. **LOU** has grazed her leg and
is deeply concerned. **PRIYA** rummages in her
bag and puts a plaster on **LOU**'s leg.)*

PRIYA. Imagine if we'd got squashed. Nobody would ever
find our dead bodies.

Unless Dorian found us.

LOU. Who?

PRIYA. Dorian. The taxi guy?! He'd definitely come to
my funeral. Do you think he'd bring all the other taxi
drivers? D'you think they'd all drive along slowly in a
line?

LOU. What?!

PRIYA. Don't think many people would come to my
funeral.

LOU. Bloody hell, Priya, course they would.

PRIYA. Nah.

LOU. A lot of people would. Especially if you were mauled
by a bull! Your family would come –

PRIYA. No chance.

My family's messed up.

LOU. Oh.

PRIYA. My mum wouldn't notice. And my dad wouldn't
care.

LOU. Course he would.

PRIYA. Nah. He's in Spain with his new family.

LOU. Oh. OK.

PRIYA. Don't look all tragic, I'm not bothered, I don't care.

(Pause.)

LOU. If it's makes you feel better, I don't have a dad either.

PRIYA. Sorry.

LOU. Dunno who he is. Julie says it's 'not relevant'. I think it is, but nobody listens to Lou.

PRIYA. That's shit, mate. Sorry.

(Pause.)

But wait! What if he's a celebrity? What if you're secretly in the Royal Family and your dad's Prince Harry?!

LOU. I wish.

(Pause.)

Families are weird.

(Pause.)

PRIYA. Is your knee OK?

*(**LOU** nods.)*

LOU. Thanks.

(She gets up.)

OK, I think we're meant to go through that wooded bit next, which is great cos I need the loo. Bog roll!

PRIYA. Oh…

LOU. …what?!

PRIYA. … I forgot the bog roll.

LOU. Haha, very funny.

PRIYA. No, I actually did.

LOU. Swear you didn't bring it.

PRIYA. Swear down. On Greta. And the polar bears.

I told you we should have bought that She-wee invention!

LOU. I don't need a wee, I need a...

(*A pause.*)

PRIYA. Shit.

LOU. Have you got a handkerchief?

PRIYA. Who has a handkerchief?!

LOU. ... I'm gonna have to use a leaf.

PRIYA. No, MANK! You can't use a LEAF! What if it's a nettle or poisonous and you rupture your butthole!?

LOU. You can't rupture your butthole with a leaf... can you?

PRIYA. Probably!

LOU. Fine. Hand me the trowel.

PRIYA. What's a trowel?

LOU. Oh God.

PRIYA. If you can't find a good leaf, you can use the spare socks.

> (**PRIYA** *moves towards* **LOU***'s bag to get the spare socks.* **LOU** *blocks her.*)

LOU. NO!

> (*She does a rainbow breath.*)

I can do it. I can do it. Greta must have pooed in the woods. I can poo in the woods. I can do it.

> (**LOU** *goes into the woods.*)

> (**PRIYA** *explores a bit.*)

(Then she sneakily turns **LOU***'s phone on.)*

(She types something into the search bar.)

(She looks at it, then goes very quiet and still.)

*(***LOU*** eventually comes back.)*

Found a big dock leaf thing, wasn't that bad. Pooed in the wild. Gold star.

*(***PRIYA*** hasn't moved.)*

PRIYA. My mum's pregnant.

LOU. What?

PRIYA. It's on her facebook status.

*(***PRIYA*** hands the phone over to her.)*

LOU. You switched my phone on? That's a total giveaway of our location, we're meant to be untraceable! We're meant to be outlaws!

*(***LOU*** quickly switches the phone off.)*

PRIYA. She didn't tell me.

LOU. Bloody hell, Priya!

PRIYA. Guess that's why Racist Mike's moved in.

LOU. Who?

PRIYA. My Mum's dickhead boyfriend, Mike. He drove down from Wigan in this massive car, and moved in with all his stuff – like war stuff, Winston Churchill and medals and everything – they're not even from his family, they're off ebay –

LOU. That's weird.

PRIYA. And he keeps coming into my room without knocking, and sitting on my bed and staring.

And –

He's a creep. That's why I had to leave.

There you go. That's why I ran away.

LOU. Did you tell your Mum?

PRIYA. She doesn't believe me! I filmed him on my phone to show her, but then Racist Mike found out, and took my phone off me he – he called me the P-word and my mum wouldn't listen to me, she only listens to him, and its BULLSHIT, and –

LOU. Oh my God, Priya.

PRIYA. She hasn't even noticed I've gone.

LOU. She probably thinks you're at Izzy's or something.

PRIYA. I've called her every day and she hasn't answered or called me back or anything.

LOU. Well she doesn't know my number, so maybe-

PRIYA. She doesn't care.

And now she's having a whole new baby with Racist Mike, so that's it. I can't go home.

LOU. But after a month, it'll be different, it'll-

PRIYA. You don't get it, do you? Julie's gonna cry and forgive you, and you'll go back to your fluffy pyjamas and your nice house, but I can't. I'll have to stay in the Peak District. I have to live in the bothy for ever and I don't even know what a bothy is!

LOU. It's a barn. Just a barn that you sleep in.

　　　　(Pause.)

PRIYA. I'm like that polar bear. Like the last one, that nobody gives a shit about.

LOU. I give a shit!

PRIYA. Don't lie! You only let me come because you didn't want me staying in your house and breaking stuff.

LOU. That's not true.

PRIYA. I'm a lost cause.

LOU. No you're not!

PRIYA. Then why did you say it?

LOU. I didn't mean –

PRIYA. I am a lost cause. I'm shit. So you can go to the bothy. And I'll stay here.

LOU. Priya –

PRIYA. Forget about me! Just let me go extinct.

> (**PRIYA** *sits on her bag and doesn't move.* **LOU** *doesn't know what to do.)*

Eight

(Time passes. It starts to get dark. **PRIYA** *remains sitting on the bag.)*

LOU. It's going to be dark soon.

(Nothing. **LOU** *pretends to leave.)*

I've got all the Pop-Tarts!

(But it doesn't work. **PRIYA** *still doesn't move.)*

We can't just.

(Nothing.)

This is getting silly now. Come on! I'll leave you here. I will!

(Still nothing.)

I'm serious, you can't just sit here. We're not polar bears, we don't have layers of fat reserves or arctic fur or whatever. If we don't keep going, when it gets dark, we'll freeze to death. And that evil bull will hunt us down and gorge on our wasted corpses!

(Still nothing.)

Priya!

We're supposed to be Shewolves! Shewolves don't give up. Shewolves... bite back!

PRIYA. I thought you were a vegan.

LOU. I know, but.

Come on! Nobody at home expects you to actually do this, Priya. You have to prove them wrong. Show them that... that you're more than just a fart in a ski suit!

(Nothing.)

I'm serious. If you die of hyperthermia, then nothing will change. Racist Mike will win.

(They look at each other.)

Please don't be a polar bear. Be a Shewolf with me.

PRIYA. This bothy better not be a shithole.

*(**PRIYA** gets up.)*

Nine

(They arrive at the bothy.)

LOU. Here we are!

You're really good at map-reading.

PRIYA. You literally just follow the lines.

LOU. Not everyone can do that.

(They put their bags down and look around.)

This is a nice bothy.

PRIYA. It's not as shit as I thought, to be fair.

(They look at the view of the countryside.)

LOU. We made it. The Peak District.

PRIYA. The PD.

LOU. The PD.

PRIYA. Kinda looks like a screensaver. A really nice peaceful one.

I get the eco thing a bit now. Think I'd be sad if everything died and the sheep started eating each other and foaming at the mouth.

LOU. I think you're confusing ecocide with a zombie apocalypse.

D'you wanna make the fire?

PRIYA. With the lighter and the tampon? Sick.

*(**PRIYA** looks for a tampon and a lighter. **LOU** gathers sticks.)*

Can I ask you something? What did you think about me – before we were Shewolves?

LOU. Um.

PRIYA. You can be honest, I've got a thick skin.

LOU. I guess I thought you were a little bit unstable. Impulsive. Not in a bad way! But like if you got a neck tattoo I wouldn't be surprised.

PRIYA. Oh my God I always wanted a neck tattoo! Like a platypus or something coming round to my mouth so when I speak its like... yeah.

LOU. What did you think of me?

PRIYA. Um.

LOU. You can tell me the truth, I don't care.

PRIYA. Just that you're dead clever. And that you're gonna be OK. Like, you'll be a really good adult.

LOU. That's really nice. Thank you.

PRIYA. I also thought you had a stick up your arse. Just a little bit.

LOU. I do, a little bit.

> *(They laugh.)*

You won't have to live here you know. We'll think of something.

> *(**PRIYA** makes a spark.)*

PRIYA. OMG I made a fire! Pass me those beans!

LOU. *(In a cave man voice.)* Beans.

PRIYA. *(In a cave man voice.)* Beans.

> *(They dance around the campfire with tins of beans.)*

PRIYA & LOU. BEANS BEANS BEANS BEANS BEANS BEANS BEANS BEANS!

Ten – A

(Music. A montage.*)

(They eat Pop-Tarts. **PRIYA** *reads the ingredients.)*

PRIYA. What's beef gelatine?

*(***LOU*** *is shocked and spits out the Pop-Tart.)*

---

* A licence to produce SHEWOLVES does not include a performance licence for any third-party or copyrighted music. Licensees should create an original composition or use music in the public domain. For further information, please see Music Use Note on page iii

Ten – B

(They jump around in sleeping bags. They invent their signature dance-move, 'The Maggot'.)

PRIYA. Be a maggot.

LOU. What?

PRIYA. Do this. Do the maggot.

LOU. I'm a maggot.

PRIYA. Now do the sexy maggot.

*(**LOU** does a crazy sexy maggot dance.)*

LOU. I'm a sexy maggot.

PRIYA. YES, SEXY MAGGOT!

Ten – C

> (**LOU** *and* **PRIYA** *hold their hands on their hearts.*)

LOU. Make a pact.

I pledge my unfaltering allegiance to the Shewolves.

PRIYA. I pledge my – can I have shorter words?

LOU. NO! You can do it! Unfaltering allegiance.

> (**PRIYA** *repeats it with her top lip tucked up over her teeth.*)

PRIYA. I pledge my unfaltering allegiance to the Shewolves.

LOU. We are Shewolves!

BOTH. We are Shewolves!

> (**LOU** *growls.* **PRIYA** *growls. They growl together. They howl together.*)

Eleven

(Night. They're both in sleeping bags.)

*(*PRIYA *sits up.)*

PRIYA. Are you awake? Have I been farting in my sleep? I have proper anxiety about that.

LOU. Not that I heard.

Or smelled.

PRIYA. If I do, it's not my fault. That was quite a lot of beans for me.

LOU. OK. Night.

PRIYA. Night.

*(*PRIYA *lies back down.)*

(They hear a farmer's car pulling up nearby.)

PRIYA & LOU. Did you hear that? / What was that?

LOU. Turn off the lamp!

Come on.

(They turn off the lamp, carefully unzip the sleeping bags and get up.)

(They peek through a hole in the door.)

PRIYA. Is that a torch? Can you see that light bobbing along?

LOU. Probably just a farmer. They have to check on cows in the night sometimes, I saw it on *Countryfile*.

PRIYA. Is it getting closer? Do you think he knows we're here?

LOU. Why would he? Everyone thinks we're in Derby.

PRIYA. ...not everyone.

LOU. ?

PRIYA. Not Dorian.

LOU. Dorian thinks we're doing D of E, he totally bought it.

PRIYA. I accidentally told him we were running away. When you were unloading the bags from the taxi. He looked at me and did a little smile and said "I ran away once" and I didn't know what to say so I just laughed and fist-bumped him.

LOU. You what?!

PRIYA. Chill out, he was sound.

LOU. We don't know that! He could be a murderer! That could be him!

PRIYA. ...he did have a weird smile.

> *(They look at each other. They are scared.)*

> *(Footsteps and torchlight start heading towards the bothy.)*

LOU. Shhhhh! He's heard us!

PRIYA. Oh my God, he's coming!

Do you really think it's Dorian? I thought Dorian had a mullet.

> *(Pause.)*

Unless he had a haircut.

> *(They watch the torch coming closer.)*

I'm gonna shit myself. Why did you make us wear ski-suits?!

(They wait, holding their breath as the torch comes right up to the door.)

LOU. Hang on.

*(**LOU** goes to her bag.)*

PRIYA. What you doing?!

LOU. Stand back.

*(**LOU** produces a taser gun.)*

PRIYA. What the fuck?!

*(**LOU** takes a deep breath and opens the door a tiny bit. She peers round it and aims the gun.)*

LOU. *(To the farmer.)* Back off, Dorian!

See this? *(She waves the gun.)* Yeah? We are ARMED! YEAH!

(The farmer legs it back to the car. He starts up the car and drives away really fast.)

He's gone.

PRIYA. WHAT THE FUCK?! Point that down! What the fuck is that?!

LOU. It's a taser gun. I made it with my 3D printer – got the pattern online.

PRIYA. You made a gun?

LOU. It's not a gun gun, it's just for zapping. For self defence!

PRIYA. Do you know how much trouble we would get in for having that?! Especially me!

LOU. It's only a taser. It just buzzes you, it doesn't harm you!

PRIYA. You're meant to to be the bigbrain, but that is bare stupid.

LOU. Well it's a good job I brought it cos I just saved us from a killer taximan.

Who else did you tell?

PRIYA. Nobody!

LOU. You gave away our location, and now somebody knows we're here. They might call the police, or come back and get us! We're not safe here anymore!

PRIYA. You brought us here! With a WEAPON! You came up with this whole crazy plan!

LOU. The plan was working! 'Til you switched the phone on because you were thinking about yourself, like you always do!

PRIYA. Someone's got to think about me!

LOU. You make everybody think about you, the entire time, because you never ever stop talking!

PRIYA. Talking's fun, I'm fun person, you should try it!

LOU. When the world stops burning, then I'll have fun, ok?!

PRIYA. No you won't, you'll just find another emergency to moan about! You have your big house, your credit card, your robot printer and a whole cupboard just for snacks!! You've got such a nice life and you spend it complaining!

LOU. Just because I have a nice house doesn't mean I have a nice life.

PRIYA. You are so smart but you don't know anything. You have no idea what it's like.

LOU. You have no idea how much danger you put us in by blabbing to Dorian!

PRIYA. I was just having a laugh with him! If you have a laugh with people, like I do, then you might actually make some friends!

LOU. I have friends. I have lots of –

PRIYA. Fuck off! You got invited to one sleepover in Year Six at Sammy's house, just so she could put your hand in water while you were asleep to make you wet yourself!

(Pause.)

LOU. *(Mortified.)* Did she tell you that?!

PRIYA. She told everyone!

LOU. That's not why she invited me.

PRIYA. Yeah, right.

LOU. We were friends.

PRIYA. You don't know how to be a friend!

LOU. Neither do you! That's why nobody likes you.

PRIYA. Yes they do.

LOU. They don't like you, they feel sorry for you, Priya, because you are a lost cause! No wonder your mum's replaced you!

*(**PRIYA** stops still.)*

(A long pause.)

*(Then **PRIYA** gets her bag.)*

What are you doing?

PRIYA. Leaving.

LOU. Now?

You can't go now, it's dark outside. It's like... midnight!

(**PRIYA** *starts throwing her stuff into her bag.*)

Where are you going?

I'm sorry. I was really nasty then, I – I didn't mean what I said, you're not a lost cause, you're –

(**PRIYA** *keeps packing.*)

You can't run away from running away! We have to stick together, that's what Shewolves do.

(**PRIYA** *goes to the door.*)

PRIYA. I don't want to be a Shewolf any more.

(**LOU** *blocks the door.*)

LOU. But we took a pledge. We made a pact.

PRIYA. I'm breaking it.

Move.

LOU. No.

PRIYA. MOVE!

(**LOU** *is shocked. She moves out of the way.*)

LOU. Wait! Take this, take the phone. Just in case.

(**PRIYA** *looks at her.*)

I know you're not really a black belt.

(**PRIYA** *takes the phone.*)

Don't go.

(*But she's gone.*)

Shit.

Twelve – A

(The bothy. Sirens in the distance. **LOU** *starts to panic. She lights a lantern, grabs her bag and the map and tries to work out where to go, but she can't read the map properly. She looks out of the window but can't see* **PRIYA** *anymore. She throws everything onto the floor.)*

Twelve – B

(Outside. **PRIYA** *walks through the field and along the track. When she gets to the top of the hill, she stops and switches the phone on. Julie has sent loads of voicemails.* **PRIYA** *hears them. They're a mixture of terror and fury. Julie has lost her shit.)*

Twelve – C

(The bothy. **LOU** *has a panic attack. The sirens and helicopters are closer.* **LOU** *tries to do rainbow breaths but she can't.)*

Twelve – D

*(Outside. **PRIYA** tries calling her mum. No answer. She tries again.)*

Twelve – E

*(The bothy. **LOU** gives up trying to scowl. She takes a deep breath, throws her head back and howls like a wolf.)*

Twelve – F

(Outside. **PRIYA** *hears* **LOU***'s howl. The phone is still ringing. Mike answers.* **LOU** *howls again.)*

*(***PRIYA** *hangs up the phone.)*

(She opens an app on the phone and starts running down the track to the bothy, as a **POLICE** *car crosses the valley.)*

Thirteen

(**LOU** *walks slowly towards the door. She takes a deep breath and stands against the door. She hears someone (***PRIYA***) outside.*)

LOU. Please don't arrest me, I don't want to die in juvie!

PRIYA. *(Out of sight.)* Lou! Shut up! It's me!

LOU. Priya?!

PRIYA. Let me in!

(*They both bundle back inside the bothy and* **PRIYA** *slams the door.*)

That was really mean.

LOU. I know.

PRIYA. Don't speak to me like that again, OK?

LOU. I'm really sorry. I am. That was. I really am sorry. You were right. There's a lot of things I don't have any idea about. But. I know you're not a lost cause.

PRIYA. You swear?

LOU. On Greta and the polar bears.

(*Pause.*)

PRIYA. OK.

I'm sorry I said you have no friends. It's cos you're a strawberry lace. People get excited about all the crazy-tasting sweets but you can't go wrong with a strawberry lace. You get me?

LOU. Um...?

PRIYA. Fizzwizz. Strawberry lace.

Anyway, listen! I've had a gold star brainwave lightbulb thing.

LOU. OK?

PRIYA. We should bite back. Instead of running away.

LOU. ?

PRIYA. That's what you said! Shewolves bite back! I was climbing this massive mountain and I switched on the phone. Julie left you loads of messages. I was hoping she was maybe gonna adopt me but she sounds quite scary actually. And then I rang my Mum and Racist Mike answered and I was like. We can't run away any more. We've got to do a Greta.

When the police get here, we're not gonna cry, we're not gonna run away. We're gonna do a protest.

LOU. What?!

PRIYA. I can film it and put it on insta. Like Greta. Or go live. Like Greta, but better.

LOU. No, Priya –

PRIYA. Nobody used to care about Greta. She was just some Swedish kid with a weird frog hat. But then, she started saying stuff online, and everyone listened. And now nobody can stop her, she's like a superhero genius eco-queen! You could do that – use big words and do the scowl and we can post it and everyone will listen. And it will be like a protest! A live protest. Like Greta, but better!

> *(Pause.)*

LOU. How are we going to do this protest, then?

PRIYA. We glue ourselves to the bothy and refuse to leave! And they won't be able to take us away without ripping off all our skin!

LOU. I didn't pack any superglue.

I guess we could make a banner, or –

PRIYA. We don't have time for craft!!

>   (*She looks around.*)

...we're gonna have to lock ourselves in. And not leave the bothy until they listen to us.

LOU. ...like a barricade?

>   (**PRIYA** *doesn't know this word.*)

Like Les Miserables?!

PRIYA. Speak English!

>   (*Four* **POLICE** *cars pull up outside.*)

LOU. Oh my God, they're here.

PRIYA. Are you in?

>   (**LOU** *hesitates.* **PRIYA** *tucks her lip above her teeth.*)

Lou, are you in?

LOU. OK, boss.

PRIYA. Do the pact. I pledge my unfaltering allegiance to this protest.

LOU. I pledge my unfaltering allegiance to this protest.

POLICE. (*Offstage.*) Come out with your hands up. Come out of the barn with your hands UP!

>   (**PRIYA** *holds up the phone.*)

PRIYA. Ready?

LOU. OK.

PRIYA. I'm filming. We're live.

(To phone camera.) I'm in the Peak District with my best mate Lou and we're gonna do a sick protest. Check it out.

(**LOU** *peeks around the door.*)

LOU. *(To* **POLICE**.*)* This is a protest… okay?

(She slams the door.)

There's actual police.

POLICE. *(Offstage.)* Louise Humberland, come out of the bothy.

LOU. Oh my God, they know its me!!

(**PRIYA** *goes to the door and peeks round it.*)

PRIYA. *(To* **POLICE**.*)* This is a protest, yeah? We're going nowhere!

POLICE. *(Offstage on walkie-talkies.)* There is another child in the bothy. IC4. IC4, five foot three… approximately fourteen years old. Wearing a purple scrunchie and a ski suit.

(Offstage.) Come out of the bothy with your hands up!

PRIYA. *(To* **POLICE**.*)* She's not coming out until… *(To* **LOU**.*)* what do you want?

LOU. Um… not to be expelled!

PRIYA. *(To* **POLICE**.*)* Lou's not leaving this bothy until she's allowed back to school.

LOU. And Mr Davies resigns.

PRIYA. *(To* **LOU**.*)* Sick.

(To **POLICE**.*)* And Mr Davies resigns, yeah? For being a KAREN! And then you can promote Miss Brown, she's nice and she's a well better teacher than Mr Davies!

LOU. You're really good at this.

PRIYA. Thanks!

(**LOU** *edges nearer to the door.*)

POLICE. *(Offstage.)* Bring out your weapons. Place them slowly at your feet and raise your hands above your heads. Do what we tell you, and you won't be in trouble.

PRIYA. Yeah, right.

(**LOU** *shouts through the door.*)

LOU. Yeah, right!! We're not leaving this bothy until... until Racist Mike gets sent back to Wigan.

PRIYA. Nice!

LOU. Or jail! And...

PRIYA. Say the climate stuff! Go on!

LOU. And we want meaningful environmental pledges from the government. NOW.

(**PRIYA** *joins her at the door and they shout their demands.*)

PRIYA. Yeah! And somebody tell Julie to chill out and stop making Lou do so much homework! This girl needs some sleepovers and a face mask!

POLICE. *(Offstage.)* This is not a negotiation. Come out of the bothy or we will smash the door down.

Place your weapons on the floor and hold your hands above your heads.

You have ten seconds.

Ten.

(*The* **POLICE** *lights get closer.*)

LOU. What do we do now?!

POLICE. *(Offstage.)* Nine.

PRIYA. I don't actually know.

POLICE. *(Offstage.)* Eight.

LOU. We've got viewers!

POLICE. *(Offstage.)* Seven.

PRIYA. *(To the phone.)* A lot of viewers! Tag your friends. Join the pack. Hashtag Shewolves.

POLICE. *(Offstage.)* Sixfivefour.

BOTH. WHAT?!

LOU. Wait.

> *(***LOU*** *runs to her bag.)*

POLICE. *(Offstage.)* Three.

PRIYA. *(To the phone.)* SHEWOLVES, SHEWOLVES!

POLICE. *(Offstage.)* Two.

> *(***PRIYA*** *and* ***LOU*** *look at each other.)*

BOTH. *(To the phone.)* SHEWOLVES, SHEWOLVES!

One.

Now!

> *(***PRIYA*** *and* ***LOU*** *charge out of the door of the bothy.)*

SHEWOLVES, MOTHERFUCKERS!!!!

> *(Lights strobe and music blasts*.* ***LOU*** *fires the taser and* ***PRIYA*** *films, the* ***POLICE*** *swamp them and everything goes dark.)*

---

* A licence to produce SHEWOLVES does not include a performance licence for any third-party or copyrighted music. Licensees should create an original composition or use music in the public domain. For further information, please see Music Use Note on page iii

Fourteen

(A credits roll montage.)*

---

* A licence to produce SHEWOLVES does not include a performance licence for any third-party or copyrighted recordings. Licensees should create their own.

Fourteen – A

(**POLICE** *custody.*)

LOU. Detective Inspector.

PRIYA. Your Majesty.

LOU. *(To* **PRIYA**.*)* He's a policeman not the King.

PRIYA. Sorry. Your highness.

LOU. *(To* **OFFICER REID**.*)* I think we all agree that taser was a mistake.

PRIYA. We didn't think it would actually fire. We're only fourteen, we got confused by the internet.

LOU. So if you could let us off with a warning, we'd be so grateful.

PRIYA. Then we can get back home to our mothers, and continue our studies.

BOTH. Thanks.

(They grin at each other.)

Fourteen – B

*(**LOU***'s living room.)*

LOU. Julie, listen. I've tried so hard to do everything like you planned, and to be exactly how you want me to be. I've tried to get full marks, I've done more homework than probably any one in the history of the world, I've been so sensible but I can't do it any more. I can't try to be perfect any more. I don't want to be perfect.

I want to have a messy bedroom and eat too much pic n mix and have sleepovers and save the planet whilst having a perfectly plucked monobrow and I need you to know that none of those things make me a bad person.

I need you to let me make mistakes.

And maybe… hang out with me. And take me to Five Guys sometimes. Just for fun.

What d'you think.

Mum?

Fourteen – C

(Careers advice at school.)

PRIYA. We've already planned our careers, Miss.

LOU. I'm studying 3D design at Uni, and Priya's getting an ice-cream van.

PRIYA. I'm gonna sell ice creams and veggie Pop-Tarts.

LOU. Miss Brown?

>   *(Pause.)*

Thanks for letting me come back to school.

PRIYA. And Miss?

I reckon you're quite good at listening. So gold star for you, Miss, nice one.

Um.

I think. I sort of. I sort of need to talk to someone.

I can talk dead fast so it won't take long, yeah?

>   *(Miss Brown listens to Priya.)*

Things. Things aren't good at home, Miss.

I kind of need your help.

Fourteen – D

(In the sun. They make a video on **PRIYA***'s phone.)*

PRIYA. We're in LA, bitches!!!

LOU. At Emma Watson's feminist summer camp.

PRIYA. Only joking, we're at Butlins with my mum and my new little sister, baby Greta. Sick name, right?

LOU. And while we're here, we're making some awesome new content for you.

PRIYA. And chilling in the pool.

LOU. We'll be posting got some eco videos and some legal advice so you can get your voice heard without getting arrested.

PRIYA. Yeah, don't get arrested.

LOU. Do not get arrested! Howl if you need anything.

PRIYA. We love you! Have fun –

LOU. And get stuff done!

BOTH. SHEWOLVES, MOTHERFUCKERS!!!

(They laugh and dance.)

End

ABOUT THE AUTHOR

Sarah Middleton is an actor/writer from Derby.

Writing includes: *Little Red Riding Hood* (Nottingham Playhouse); The *Wishing Stone* (Separate Doors/ Derby Theatre/Chichester Festival Theatre); *Wilf Goes Wild* (MPTheatricals) and *Pinocchio* (Nottingham Playhouse).

Acting includes: *The Hypocrite* (RSC/Hull Truck); *Pomona* (National Theatre, Royal Exchange and Orange Tree); *Treasure Island* (Birmingham Rep); *Hunter Killer* (Millennium Films/Netflix); *Coronation Street* (ITV) and *Midsummer Murders* (ITV).

Sarah is an Associate Writer of Middle Child Theatre Company, a recipient of a Peggy Ramsay Grant and a Hosking Houses residency through Mercury Musical Developments. In 2022 she was awarded a National Theatre Peter Shaffer commission to write a new play, *Chuckers*, for Derby Theatre. *SHEWOLVES* is Sarah's first full-length play. She co-runs Shewolves Productions with Hannah Stone. They are currently developing a thriller with skateboarding; *Darkslide*.

9 780573 133671